Where Animals Live

The World of Ants

Words by Virginia Harrison

Adapted from Linda Losito's *The Ant on the Ground*

**Photographs by
Oxford Scientific Films**

Gareth Stevens Publishing
Milwaukee

Contents

Ants and Where They Live	3	Raising the Young	18
Ants Around the World	4	Ants and Plants	20
The Ant's Body	6	Ant Neighbors and Uninvited Guests	22
The Life of the Colony	8	Ant Enemies	24
Nest Building	10	Protection from Enemies	26
Food and Feeding	12	Ants and People	28
Predatory or Hunting Ants	14	The Ant on the Ground	30
Mating and Egg Laying	16	Index and New Words About Ants	32

Note: The use of a capital letter for an ant's name means that it is a *species* of ant (for example, Australian Honeypot Ant). The use of a lowercase, or small, letter means that it is a member of a larger *group* of ants.

Ants and Where They Live

Ants are found almost everywhere, and in almost every kind of *habitat*. They can't live in the severe cold of the North and South poles. But otherwise, where there is food, there are ants. They spend their lives in a constant cycle of searching for, carrying, and storing food and nesting materials (above).

Ants carry large quantities of dead leaves, animals, and insects into their underground nests for food. These carpenter ants from North America are eating a dead tent caterpillar.

Ants are insects and belong to the same group as bees and wasps. All the insects in this group — including mating ants — have transparent wings.

Ants Around the World

Ants thrive in all parts of the world, probably because they cooperate in food gathering and nest building. They live in colonies that have varying numbers of *workers*. There are about 10,000 *species* of ants living around the world.

Especially large numbers of ants live in the tropics. African weaver ants (above) build their nests out of leaves that are still attached to the trees, gluing the leaves together with a sticky silk from the head glands of an ant *larva*.

These Australian Honeypot Ant workers hang from the roof of their nest while other workers fill them with *honeydew*. To prepare for a food shortage, the ants gather honeydew and fill each worker's *crop*. The rest of the colony will take droplets from the mouths of these swollen storage ants until they return to normal size.

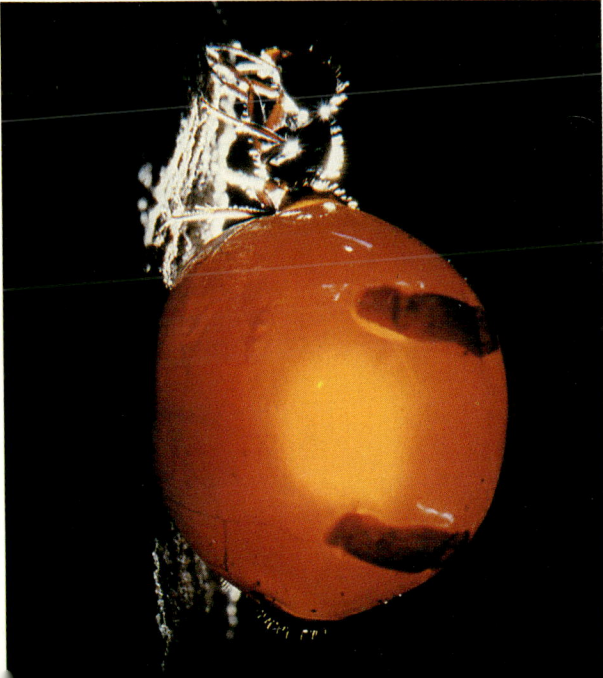

The Ant's Body

The ant has a typical insect body, with three main parts: the head, *thorax*, and *abdomen*.

On the head is a mouth, two *antennae*, and two *compound eyes*. The eyes are made of many small sections called facets. Each facet acts like an individual *eye*. The driver ant of Africa uses its antennae in place of eyes. Some ants have simple *eyes*, called *ocelli*, that only detect light.

The ant's skeleton is on the outside of its body. It is called an *exoskeleton* and is made of a tough substance called chitin.

Army ants have a special group of soldiers that protects the smaller workers with their huge jaws.

The size and form of ant species vary. The Tic-tac Ant (below) has an unusually long, thin body. But ants are generally built the same. The thorax has six legs, each with several sections for flexible movement. Male ants and young *queen* ants have wings and mate in the air. Between the thorax and abdomen, there is a small waist. The abdomen holds the ant's stomach, waste system, and sex organs. Males have *testes*, which produce *sperm*, and females have *ovaries*, which produce eggs. Some have stingers with which they poison their *prey*.

The Life of the Colony

Like many bees and wasps, ants live together in family groups called colonies. This army ant queen is swollen with eggs. The queen is the largest of all the ants in the colony, and her only purpose is to lay eggs. She produces a chemical called *queen substance*, which the worker ants lick and pass around the colony. This tells them that she is fit and healthy.

⬆ Larger worker ants collect food, while smaller workers tend the nest, care for the young, and feed the queen. The ants above are waiting to catch female fungus gnats that come to lay eggs.

Large colonies have one or more fertile queens, thousands of sterile worker females, and several hundred males. There are fewer males than females, as the males' only purpose is to mate with the queens. They die soon after mating.

The entire colony works together as a team. ⬅ These army ants form a living bridge so that other ants can cross safely to another log.

Nest Building

Most ants build nests. Some build large, permanent nests, like these circular walled nests of the Mulga Ant of central Australia (above). Others build small, temporary nests in hollow plant stems, nuts, or even snail shells.

Ants on the move, like the African driver ant, dig tunnels in the ground as temporary camps called bivouacs. These South American army ants cluster together under the shelter of a log (right). Both driver ants and army ants protect their queen and larvae at the center of the nest.

European red ants pile the dug-up soil into mounds above their tunnels when the weather is warm. They put their larvae in these mounds. The warmth of the soil speeds the development of the larvae. Wood ant nests are thatched with pine needles or twigs, which help keep out the wind and rain.

One African species does not build nests, but lives in old termite nests. The worker ants are blind and quite tiny. They rarely leave the nest, but some cling to the leg hairs of the far larger queen when she leaves to start a new colony.

Food and Feeding ⬆

Most ant species are vegetarian, eating only plants. Some collect pollen, nectar from flowers (above), and juices from overripe fruit. One way ants obtain liquid food is by collecting honeydew. Tiny insects called aphids tap into plants for sugary sap. Some of the sap passes out of the aphids as drops of honeydew. Ants collect this from the aphids and in turn protect the aphids from ladybugs and other *predators* (below).

⬇

Leaf-cutter ants of Central and South America carry leaves and flower petals over their backs. They look as if they are carrying umbrellas, so they are sometimes called parasol ants!

Once back in the nest, leaf-cutters chew the leaves and petals into small pieces and let a special fungus grow on these pieces. The ants then eat the fungus.

Harvester ants live in many parts of the world and gather seeds for food. The ants mix the seeds with their saliva, creating a sugary substance called ant bread.

Predatory or Hunting Ants

Some ants are predatory and hunt other animals — even other ants! Because most predatory ants hunt alone, they can only take small pieces of larger prey back to the nest. They may drag the load backward. Or they may send for more workers to break the prey into smaller pieces for easier carrying.

Ants often prefer one type of prey, such as earthworms or caterpillars. But blind tropical army ants are not choosy. They stream across the forest floor, attacking any animal in their path. Usually preying on small insects, they will also devour a sleeping python, or even take apart a horse that is tied and cannot escape!

Many insects have built-in protection from ants. Some hide, others have protective coats, and still others release a repulsive chemical. Unprotected insects, such as this wasp grub, may be quickly covered and carried away in a "cradle" of workers.

Mating and Egg Laying

When the old queen begins to make less queen substance, the workers know it is time to produce more queens and males. They feed extra food to some of the female larvae, thus causing them to grow larger.

When they emerge from the nest, male ants have wings (above), as do the queens (below).

Males gather in groups when the queen is ready to mate. Sometimes they even fight to mate with her. As she flies close, one male will fly out and mate with her in midair or on the ground (below). After mating, queens shed their wings.

Some queens wait till spring to start their colonies. Others search right away for warm soil in which to dig an egg chamber. The queen lays several thousand tiny white bean-shaped eggs. These eggs are in the first stage in the life cycle of an ant. They hatch as larvae, develop into *pupae*, and finally become adults.

Raising the Young

All ants, even queens (above), guard their eggs and larvae. When a nest is disturbed, workers pick them up and carry them to a safer place.

Worker ants constantly tend the eggs, larvae, and pupae (below). They lick the eggs to keep them clean and moist. They groom, move, and feed the larvae. As time passes, larvae molt their skins several times. Each new skin marks a new stage. The old and young larvae smell and feel different. This signals the ants to feed them different foods. Workers *regurgitate* liquid food to feed younger larvae.

Large pieces of meat or seeds can be fed to third-stage larvae. The workers soften the food with saliva. Eventually, larvae go into a resting stage, called a pupa, where they push off the final larval skin and form a hard shell (above).

While in the pupal stage, the body breaks down and rebuilds into an adult ant. So if you break open an early pupa, all you see is a thick yellow liquid! Ants that do not remain in one place must transport their pupae (below). Once fully developed, the adult chews its way out of the shell. It has now completed its *metamorphosis*.

Ants and Plants

Some trees produce nectar in bumps on the stalks of the flower. These trees are often covered with ants. In return for the nectar, the ants keep the tree free of leaf-eating insects.

In Africa and South America, Thorny Acacia trees are home to ant colonies. Some thorns swell and become hollow, and recently mated queens chew into the thorns to begin a new colony there. Worker ants defend the colony from any insect that may land on the tree.

Ants have another way of protecting the tree, and thus the colony itself. Like gardeners, they cut down any new plants near the base of the tree that might crowd out the tree. In return, the Acacia trees produce leaf growths rich in oil and protein, and the ants collect them for food.

These leaf-cutter ants from Trinidad tend an underground garden of edible fungus. The fungus grows on pieces of leaves that the ants have gathered and chewed up.

Ant Neighbors and Uninvited Guests

These ants are not eating the caterpillars. They are eating sweet juices that the caterpillars secrete. In return, the caterpillars are protected from predators and take food from the ants' nest. They form a relationship that helps both sides, like that between these ants and these treehoppers.

Caterpillars and other insects may use the juices they secrete to trick ants into taking them into the ants' nests — even while these insects may be eating the ants' own larvae!

Insects may also fool ants and get into the nest by looking or smelling like ant larvae. Once in the nest, some insects even cling to the queen's abdomen and eat the eggs as they are laid.

Insects can also use the ant's communication system to take food. A rove beetle "talks" an ant out of a drop of nectar by tapping it on the back.

Common Black Ants are fooled by the larval appearance of flat white wood lice. But if a wood louse is knocked on its back, an ant will recognize it right away and kill it.

Ant Enemies

Ants are never safe from their many enemies. The anteater (above) and the Scaly Armadillo, both of South America, and the pangolin of Africa are all adapted for preying on ants. They have big, heavy claws to destroy nests, and long, sticky tongues that scoop up ants.

Other animals, such as frogs, toads, lizards, and birds like the woodpecker, also have long, sticky tongues that can snatch a mouthful of ants with each quick lick.

Spiders are silent ant predators that drop down on silken threads and wrap the ant into a bundle.

Ants are hosts to several kinds of *parasites* in or on their bodies. Mites suck ant blood from the surface, while tiny roundworms may bore inside the skins of ant larvae. With the mite living inside it, the ant fails to grow properly as an adult.

The ferocious ant lion is the larval stage of the delicate lacewing. It builds funnel-shaped traps and catches unsuspecting ants with its huge jaws.

Protection from Enemies

A small, fragile insect, the ant defends itself and its nest with a combination of poison and pain.

The bulldog ant from Australia is a biter and a stinger. Its head has sharply toothed jaws (below left), and its abdomen has a powerful stinger (below right). Bulldog ants grip their victims with their jaws as they sting them from behind. They may use these weapons when threatened or when killing prey.

▲
A sting from the South American Fire Ant causes a burning sensation. Here, a mass of Fire Ants floats across the water. The mass rolls over and over so the ants can breathe.

One of the most powerful insect poisons known comes from the large harvester ant of North and South America. The poison spreads through the bloodstream of its victim, causing extreme pain. It can kill humans.

The "exploding ant" has perhaps the most unusual defense. When the ant is threatened, its abdomen blows up!

Ants and People

For centuries, ants have shared the same buildings in which people live and work. One such ant, the Pharaoh's Ant, normally lives in the tropics. Yet it has made its way into the bakeries, cafeterias, and hospitals of northern regions. These places are warm and full of food, and the ants live in heating vents.

The ant also lives in our homes as a pest. But the tale of the grasshopper and the ant reminds us of its boundless energy when gathering and storing food. And to some people, ants are a tasty treat — especially chocolate-covered ants!

The ant's most important job for humans, though, is to kill pests that destroy our crops and cause disease. Ants that nest in Acacia trees destroy young plants that compete for
← space with the Acacia (opposite, left). This helps the Acacia flourish. Some ants eat whole
← flowers (opposite, right). This keeps plants from making seeds. But ants also keep out caterpillars and insects that lay eggs in flowers and prevent seed production.

The sad story of the energetic ant and the lazy grasshopper, as illustrated in this poem about an ant and a cicada published in French in 1906.

29

The Ant on the Ground

Ants work hard and seem very well organized as they search for food. They depend on plants and other animals for their food, while other plants and animals in turn depend on them. Ants are an important link in the cycle known as a food chain.

Food Chain

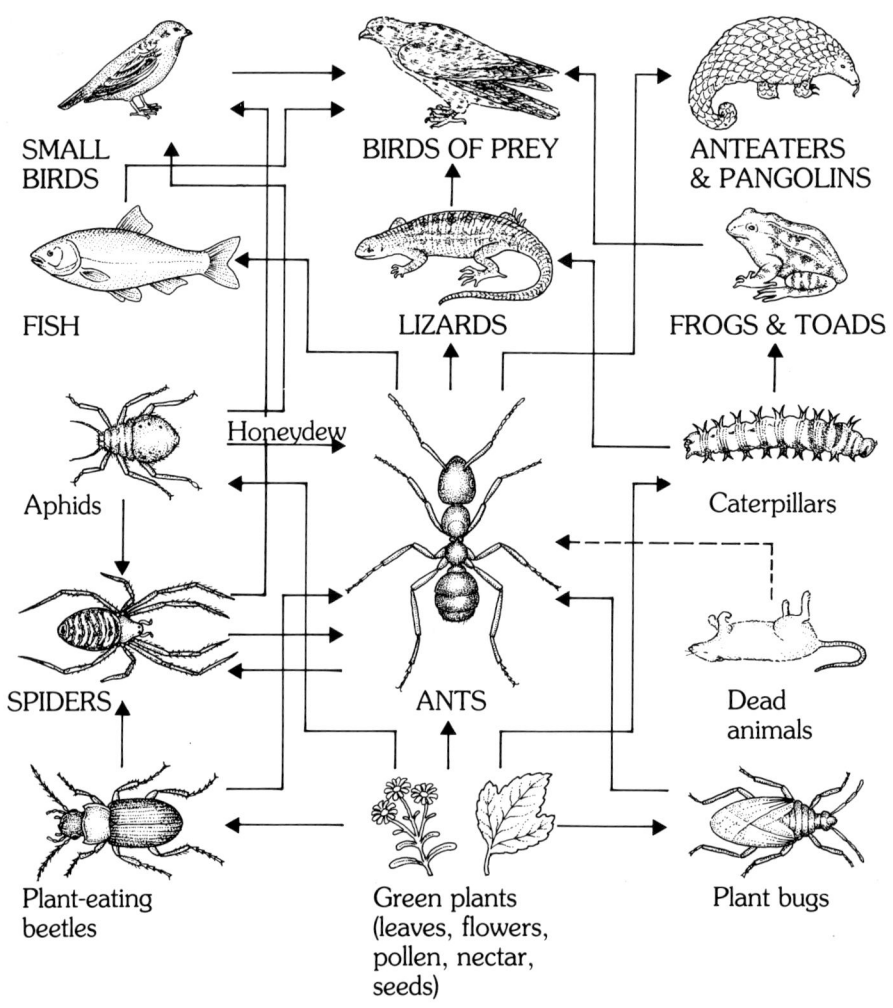

These African driver ants form a never-ending, living stream across the forest floor. Like all ants, they take nutrition from plants and animals which they eat and pass back into the soil.

Ants adapt well to their environment, use many different food sources, and reproduce in great numbers. They also survive most of the damage humans can do to the environment. As a group, ants are tough, hardy animals. They have been around for many centuries, and they are certain to survive for centuries to come.

Index and New Words About Ants

These new words about ants appear in the text on the pages shown after each definition. Each new word first appears in the text in *italics*, just as it appears here.

abdomen ...... third section of an insect's body. **6, 7, 23, 26**

antennae ...... two feelers on an ant's head sensitive to touch and smell. **6**

compound eyes .... eyes made of separate sections called facets. **6**

crop .... a special sac in the gut of an ant. **5**

exoskeleton .. tough outer skin to which muscles are attached. **6**

habitat .... place where an animal or plant normally lives. **3**

honeydew ..... mixture secreted by plant-sucking bug. **5, 12**

larva (larvae) .. young stage of insect that hatches from egg. **4, 10, 11, 16-19, 23, 25**

metamorphosis ...... change in body between young and adult stages. **19**

ocelli .... simple, light-sensitive eyes. **6**

ovaries .... structures that make eggs in females. **7**

parasite .... organism that takes its food from living tissues of another organism. **25**

predator .... an animal that kills and eats other creatures. **12, 14, 22, 25**

prey .... animal hunted for food by another. **7, 14, 15, 26**

pupa (pupae) . stage in insect life cycle where larval tissues change to adult tissues. **17-19**

queen .... fertile egg-laying female of social wasps, bees, and ants. **7-11, 16-18, 20, 23**

queen substance ..... chemical secreted by queen to prevent production of new queens by workers. **8, 16**

regurgitate .... to bring food back into the mouth from the stomach before digestion and pass it out of the body. **18**

species .... a particular kind of animal or plant. **2, 4, 7, 11, 12**

sperm .... male sex cells that are used to fertilize a female's egg. **7**

testes .... structures that make sperm in males. **7**

thorax .... middle section of body. **6, 7**

workers .... sterile female insects that do all the work. **4, 5, 7-9, 11, 15, 16, 18-20**

Reading level analysis: FRY 3, FLESCH 91 (very easy), RAYGOR 3.5, FOG 4, SMOG 3

Library of Congress Cataloging-in-Publication Data
Harrison, Virginia, 1966-
  The world of ants / words by Virginia Harrison ; adapted from Linda Losito's The ant on the ground ; photographs by Oxford Scientific Films.
    p. cm. -- (Where animals live)
  Summary: Simple text and illustrations depict the lives of ants in their natural setting describing how they feed, defend themselves, and breed.
  ISBN 0-8368-0136-9
  1. Ants--Juvenile literature. [1. Ants.] I. Losito, Linda. Ant on the ground. II. Oxford Scientific Films. III. Title. IV. Series.
QL568.F7H27   1989
595.79'6--dc20   89-4466

North American edition first published in 1989 by Gareth Stevens, Inc., 7317 West Green Tree Road, Milwaukee, WI 53223, USA. US edition, this format, copyright © by Belitha Press Ltd. Text copyright © 1989 by Gareth Stevens, Inc. All rights reserved. No part of this book may be reproduced in any form or by any means without permission in writing from Gareth Stevens, Inc. First conceived, designed, and produced by Belitha Press Ltd., London, as **The Ant on the Ground,** with an original text copyright by Oxford Scientific Films. Format copyright by Belitha Press Ltd.
Series Editor: Mark J. Sachner.   Art Director: Treld Bicknell.   Design: Naomi Games.   Line Drawings: Lorna Turpin.

The publishers wish to thank the following for permission to reproduce copyright material: **Oxford Scientific Films Ltd.** for title page, pp. 8 both, 11, 14 below, 16 below, 18 both, 19 below, 21, 22 below, 29 (J. A. L. Cooke); pp. 2, 12 below (D. R. Specker); p. 3 (Barrie Watts); p. 4 (Waina Cheng); pp. 5 above, 10, 26 right (Mantis Wildlife Films); p. 5 below (Densey Clyne); p. 6 (G. I. Bernard); p. 7 above (Raymond Mendez); p. 7 below, 9, 28 right (OSF); front cover, p. 12 above (Gerald Thompson); p. 13 (Richard K. LaVal); p. 14 above (Alastair Shay); p. 15 (M. P. L. Fogden); pp. 16 above, 19 above (Peter O'Toole); p. 17 (Tim Shepherd); pp. 20, 28 left (Philip Sharpe); p. 22 above (David Thompson); p. 24 (Breck P. Kent); p. 25 (Wallace Kirkland); p. 26 left (Kathie Atkinson); p. 27 (C. C. Lockwood); p. 31 (P. & W. Ward); back cover (Animals Animals — George K. Bryce); Partridge Productions for p. 23.

Printed in the United States of America
1 2 3 4 5 6 7 8 9 95 94 93 92 91 90 89
For a free color catalog describing Gareth Stevens' list of high-quality children's books call 1 (800) 433-0942